AMERICAN PRESIDENTS

Donald Trump

by Alex Monroe

BELLWETHER MEDIA • MINNEAPOLIS, MN

Blastoff! Readers are carefully developed by literacy experts to build reading stamina and move students toward fluency by combining standards-based content with developmentally appropriate text.

Level 1 provides the most support through repetition of high-frequency words, light text, predictable sentence patterns, and strong visual support.

Level 2 offers early readers a bit more challenge through varied sentences, increased text load, and text-supportive special features.

Level 3 advances early-fluent readers toward fluency through increased text load, less reliance on photos, advancing concepts, longer sentences, and more complex special features.

★ **Blastoff! Universe**

Reading Level

Grade **K**

Grades **1–3**

Grade **4**

This edition first published in 2022 by Bellwether Media, Inc.

No part of this publication may be reproduced in whole or in part without written permission of the publisher. For information regarding permission, write to Bellwether Media, Inc., Attention: Permissions Department, 6012 Blue Circle Drive, Minnetonka, MN 55343.

Library of Congress Cataloging-in-Publication Data

Names: Monroe, Alex (Writer of children's books) author.
Title: Donald Trump / by Alex Monroe.
Description: Minneapolis, MN : Bellwether Media, 2022. | Series: Blastoff! Readers: American Presidents | Includes bibliographical references and index. | Audience: Ages 5-8 | Audience: Grades 2-3 | Summary: "Relevant images match informative text in this introduction to Donald Trump. Intended for students in kindergarten through third grade"-- Provided by publisher.
Identifiers: LCCN 2021011387 (print) | LCCN 2021011388 (ebook) | ISBN 9781644875131 (library binding) | ISBN 9781648344817 (paperback) | ISBN 9781648344213 (ebook)
Subjects: LCSH: Trump, Donald, 1946---Juvenile literature. | Presidents--United States--Biography--Juvenile literature. | Businessmen--United States--Biography--Juvenile literature. | Celebrities--United States--Biography--Juvenile literature.
Classification: LCC E913 .M66 2022 (print) | LCC E913 (ebook) | DDC 973.933092 [B]--dc23
LC record available at https://lccn.loc.gov/2021011387
LC ebook record available at https://lccn.loc.gov/2021011388

Editor: Elizabeth Neuenfeldt   Designer: Josh Brink

Printed in the United States of America, North Mankato, MN.

Table of Contents

Who Is Donald Trump?

Donald Trump was the 45th United States president. He served from 2017 to 2021.

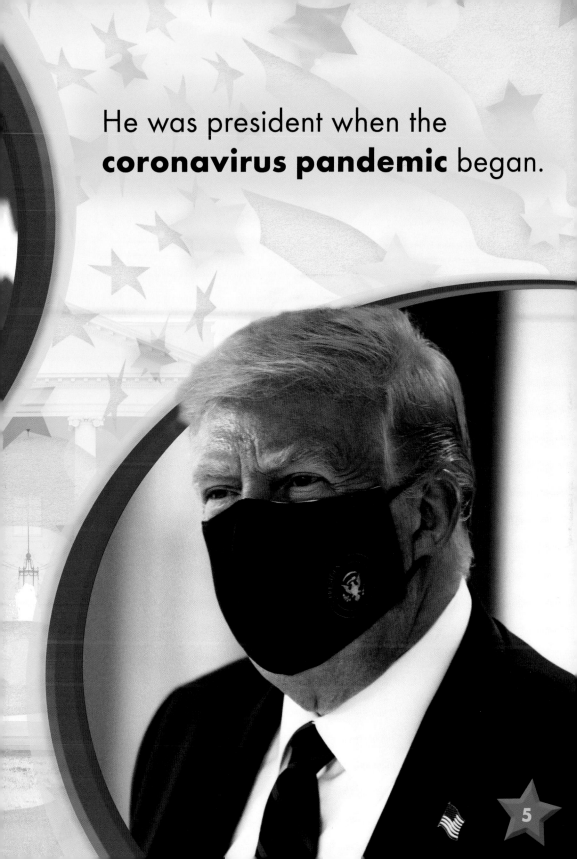

He was president when the **coronavirus pandemic** began.

5

Donald's Hometown

New York City,
New York

Donald was born in 1946.
He lived in New York City.

He often made trouble at school. He was sent to military school.

Afterward, Donald went to college. He studied **economics**. Then, he joined his father's **real estate** business.

Presidential Picks

Book

All Quiet on the Western Front

Foods

meatloaf, steak, and cherry vanilla ice cream

Sport

golf

Movie

Citizen Kane

He made a lot of money.
He became famous.

Donald looked for other projects. He had his own TV show.

Some people wanted Donald in **politics**. In 2016, he ran for president. He won!

Donald receiving a Hollywood star

DONALD TRUMP

HOLLYWOOD WALK OF FAME

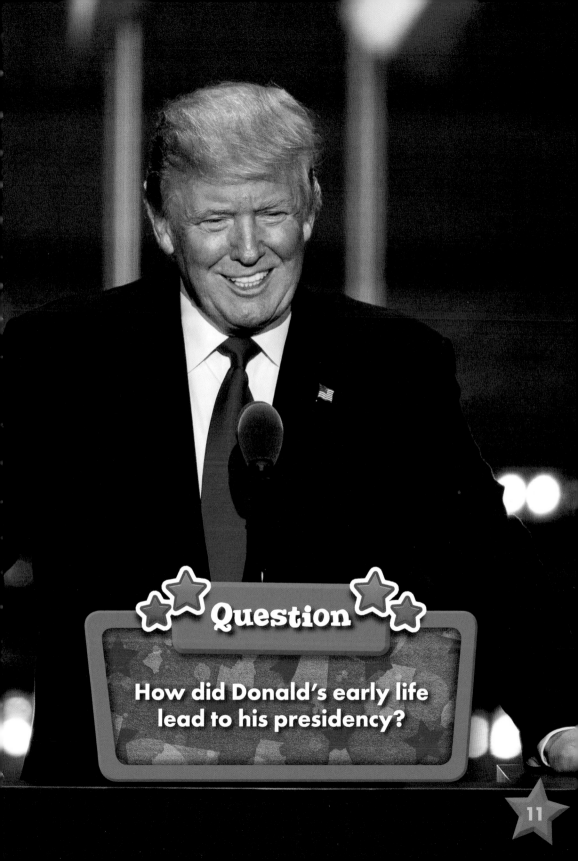

Question

How did Donald's early life lead to his presidency?

Donald took office in 2017. He began passing laws to limit **immigration**.

In June, he said the U.S. would leave the **Paris Agreement**. In December, he cut **taxes**.

Presidential Profile

Place of Birth

New York City, New York

Birthday

June 14, 1946

Schooling

Fordham University and University of Pennsylvania

Term

2017 to 2021

Party

Republican

Signature

Vice President

Mike Pence

13

In 2019, Donald was **impeached**. He **abused** his powers as president.

He was found not **guilty**.

The coronavirus pandemic hit the U.S. in 2020. Aid was slow. Many lost their lives. Others lost jobs and homes.

Donald ran for president again. He lost.

Cumulative COVID-19 Tests
JULY 20, 2020

Donald speaking about the coronavirus pandemic

2021 attack on
U.S. Capitol

Donald said he won. Many people
believed him. In 2021, some of
Donald's supporters attacked the
U.S. **Capitol**. People blamed
Donald. He was impeached again.
He was found not guilty.

Donald Timeline

November 8, 2016

Donald Trump is elected president

June 1, 2017

Donald says the U.S. will leave the Paris Agreement

December 22, 2017

Donald signs a new tax bill into law

December 18, 2019

Donald is impeached for abuse of power

November 7, 2020

Donald loses reelection

January 13, 2021

Donald is impeached for his role in the attack on the Capitol

January 20, 2021

Donald leaves office

19

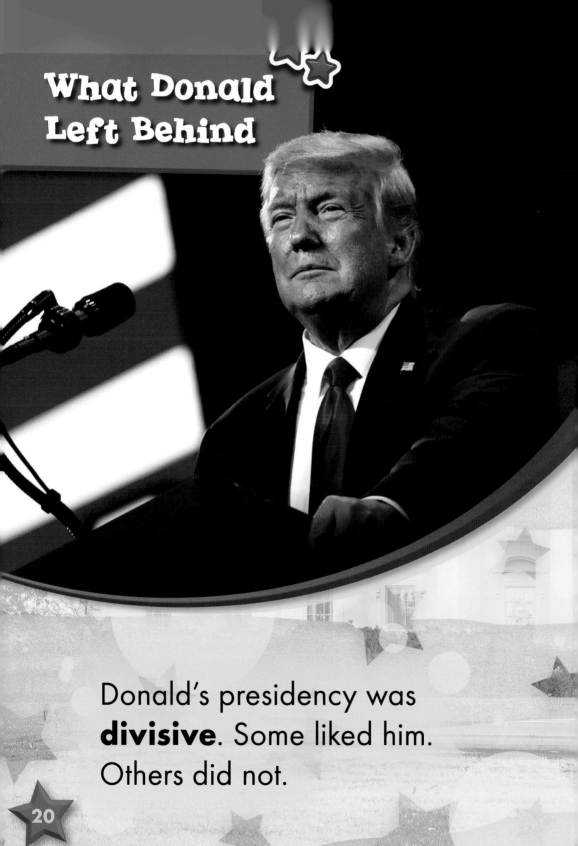

What Donald Left Behind

Donald's presidency was **divisive**. Some liked him. Others did not.

Donald changed the U.S. It will take many years to see his full **legacy**!

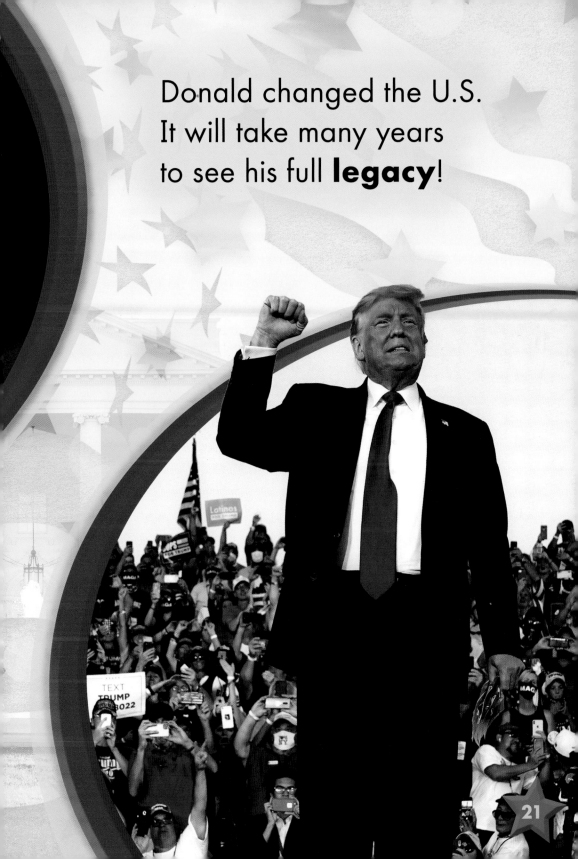

Glossary

abused—used wrongly

Capitol—a building in Washington, D.C. where the U.S. government meets

coronavirus pandemic—an outbreak of the COVID-19 virus starting in December 2019 that led to millions of deaths and shutdowns around the world

divisive—tending to cause disagreement between people

economics—the study of making, selling, and using goods and services

guilty—responsible for doing something bad or wrong

immigration—the act of people moving to live in a new country

impeached—charged with a crime done while in office

legacy—something left behind

Paris Agreement—an agreement between many countries to make efforts to fight climate change; climate change is a human-caused change in Earth's weather due to warming temperatures.

politics—the activities associated with governing

real estate—relating to the business of selling land and buildings

taxes—money paid to the government

To Learn More

AT THE LIBRARY

Rustad, Martha E. H. *The President of the United States.*
North Mankato, Minn.: Pebble, 2020.

Shamir, Ruby. *What's the Big Deal About Elections.* New
York, N.Y.: Philomel Books, 2018.

Wheeler, Jill C. *Donald Trump.* Minneapolis, Minn.:
Abdo Publishing, 2020.

ON THE WEB

FACTSURFER

Factsurfer.com gives you
a safe, fun way to find
more information.

1. Go to www.factsurfer.com.

2. Enter "Donald Trump" into the search box
   and click 🔍.

3. Select your book cover to see a list
   of related content.

Index

The images in this book are reproduced through the courtesy of: White house photo by Shealah Craighead/ Wikimedia Commons, cover; MARVIN GENTRY/ Alamy, p. 3; White House Photo/ Alamy, pp. 4, 12; ABACAPRESS/ Alamy, p. 5; Planetpix/ Alamy, p. 7; mongione, p. 8 (books); Marian Weyo, p. 8 (steak); Daxiao Production, p. 8 (golf); Pictorial Press/ Alamy, p. 8 (Citizen Kane); Bachrach/ Contributor/ Getty Images, p. 9; M. Tran/ Staff/ Getty Images, p. 10; Richard Ellis/ Alamy, pp. 10-11; Executive Office of the President of the United States/ Wikimedia Commons, p. 13 (Mike Pence); Donald Trump, Connormah/ Wikimedia Commons, p. 13 (signature); UPI/ Alamy, p. 14; 2020 Images/ Alamy, p. 15; Alex Edelman/ Alamy, p. 16; Geopix/ Alamy, p. 16-17; Brent Stirton/ Staff/ Getty Images, p. 18; Max Elram, p. 19 (Donald impeached); Media Punch/ Alamy, p. 19 (Donald leaves office); Nuno21, p. 20; Stratos Brilakis, p. 21; chrisdorney, p. 23.